For the Staubs' piano that Deborah, Jonathan, Rebecca, and Abigail might peruse*...

Love,
M R B

PENGUIN BOOKS

FROM BACH TO VERSE

During and after her ten-year concert career Josefa Heifetz married, whelped, and divorced. Since then, she has supplemented her musical life as a composer and teacher by constructing puzzles: the newspaper feature "Calculator Capers," anagrams, palindromes, crosswords, and Double-Crostics. In addition to writing light verse and collecting lexicographic curiosities (*Mrs. Byrne's Dictionary of Unusual, Obscure, and Preposterous Words*), she holds the 1974 record (as yet unbeaten) for the highest single-scoring hypothetical Scrabble play. Her age, education, hobbies, and peculiarities are of interest only to herself and certain of her immediate neighbors.

* And their dear spouses, also...

D1500648

From Bach to Verse

Comic Mnemonics for Famous Musical Themes

JOSEFA HEIFETZ

PENGUIN BOOKS

PENGUIN BOOKS
Published by the Penguin Group
Viking Penguin Inc., 40 West 23rd Street, New York, New York 10010, U.S.A.
Penguin Books Ltd, 27 Wrights Lane, London W8 5TZ, England
Penguin Books Australia Ltd, Ringwood, Victoria, Australia
Penguin Books Canada Ltd, 2801 John Street,
Markham, Ontario, Canada L3R 1B4
Penguin Books (N.Z.) Ltd, 182–190 Wairau Road,
Auckland 10, New Zealand

Penguin Books Ltd, Registered Offices:
Harmondsworth, Middlesex, England

First published 1983

7 9 10 8 6

LIBRARY OF CONGRESS CATALOGING IN PUBLICATION DATA
Heifetz, Josefa.
From Bach to verse.
1. Music—Poetry. 2. Music—Anecdotes, facetiae,
satire, etc. 3. Music—Memorizing. I. Title.
ML64.H5   1983   780′.92′2   82-24687
ISBN 0 14 00.6691 8

Printed in the United States of America
Set in Goudy Bold and Goudy Old Style

Musical notation by Eugene Wolf

Foreword

The inspiration for this collection came in the form of a dreadful performance of Schubert's Seventh which I heard on my car radio while dodging potholes on a county-maintained road. It was the funereal pace of the scherzo that did it. I was weaned on Toscanini's idea of *vivace*, which, as I recall, approached the speed of light. (That he managed to articulate each note was another measure of his genius.) Having once tasted the joys of such exhilarating *tempi*, it is quite impossible to be satisfied with anything *meno mosso*. So, in my frustration, I started to improvise lyrics and sing along: "If it's possible to sing it/ While mouthing lyrics like these,/Then the tempo's not vivace/(And Schubert wasn't Viennese)."

Although the primary intent is to entertain, these verses might serve as mnemonics for those who suffer with embarrassment while trying to match author to opus. I know I'll never again forget Franck's D Minor, or other lesser beauties by Gounod, Ippolitoff-Ivanoff, Kreisler, Offenbach, and Weber. According to certain memory experts, the more ridiculous the mnemonic, the better it serves. On the other hand, logic and reason have their groupies as well. Both camps are represented here.

Consistency is deliberately lacking except for one thing: *each syllable is sung to a single note*, so there should be no confusion about prosody. In most cases the stress points are obvious, both musically and lyrically. As a matter of fact, I can't think of a single exception, but I'm sure somebody will. Somebody usually does. And it's usually a relative.

From Bach to Verse

Bach: Bourrée

from VIOLIN PARTITA NO. 1

**Bach wrote for violin all alone
For reasons that are totally unknown.**

Bach: Jesu, Joy of Man's Desiring

There are many more Bachs
Than most people imagine:
The best known is
Johann Sebastian.

Also, there's Johann Christoph,
Johann Michael,
Carl Philipp Emanuel,
Johann Christoph Friedrich,
Johann Christian,
Wilhelm Friedemann,
Anna Magdalena.
And that's all I know
Of the various Bachs.

Bach: Two-Part Invention No. 8

Not all inventions head
For the patent office.
Some get played, instead.

Beethoven: Für Elise

Why did Ludwig write this awful piece?
  It wasn't free,
    That was for süre.

The money (all in cash) came from Elise.
  Thus it was she
    He wrote it für.

Beethoven: Symphony No. 5

Take out the trash,
Don't let it splash.

Take out the swill,
Don't let it spill,
That takes some skill.

Take out the dross,
You're not my boss,
My gain; your loss.

Take out the dregs,
Don't drop the eggs.
Too late to stop,
Go get the mop.
Take out the
God
Damned
Slop.

Beethoven: Symphony No. 9

Sigmund Freude*
Never hoid a
Concert, due to chronic slouch.

All his ritzy
(Somewhat schizy)
Patients tied him to his couch.

* Sung with two syllables, as in the original.

Beethoven: Violin Concerto in D

Don't play chess with your daughter.
She knows more than you taught her.

Berlioz: Symphonie Fantastique

Most people rate
Berlioz as great,
But, surely, not fantastic.

Bizet: L'Arlésienne

Georges Bizet
Thought pinot chardonnay
Had more bouquet
Than vin rosé
  Or Manischewitz.

Borodin: Prince Igor

Borodin
 Was a chemist with winning ways.
He wrote with the aid of gin
 On Sundays and holidays.

Brahms: Piano Concerto No. 2

Playing Brahms
  With apprehension,
Hurts your horn,
  If it's a French one.

Brahms: Symphony No. 1

The sandwich that Plato
   Thought worthy of any god
Was bacon, tomato,
   And slices of avocad-
      o.

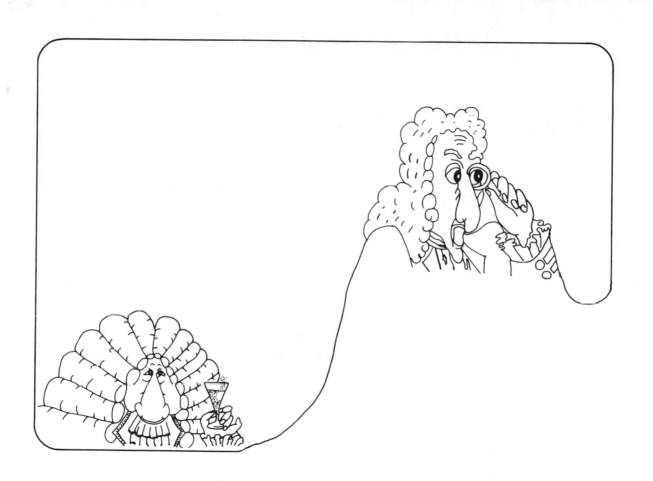

Brahms: Symphony No. 4

One seldom hears,
At junior proms,
The music of
Johannes Brahms.

His themes
   Can touch the stars.
The notes go on
   For bars and bars.
And when we've heard
   The final cadence of the score
   We still want more
   (In French: encore).

Chopin: Piano Sonata in B♭ Minor
(Funeral March)

Scales cramp my style,
Hanon is vile,
   Playing Chopin
Makes the practicing worthwhile.

Chopin: Polonaise in A

Mayonnaise
Is not as good as Hollandaise.
Hollandaise
Is inferior to Sauce Bernaise.

Chopin: Prelude No. 7

The sun gives only glare,
The moon has lost its clair.
My latest love affair
Has turned to mal de mer.
My car's beyond repair,
Likewise my thinning hair.
The vin I stashed somewhere
Stayed young and ordinaire.

Debussy: Golliwogg's Cake Walk
from THE CHILDREN'S CORNER

"Funny, you don't look Jewish,"
Said God to Moses one Saturday.

Dvořák: Humoresque

In Czechoslovakia
There lived a man named Antonin,
Whose last name can't be spelled, much less pronounced.

Dvořák: Symphony No. 5
(New World)

**Don't decide
Suicide.
Go to Mexico.**

**Have a ball,
Eat it all.*
What a way to go!**

* Suggested by my dear teacher, Darius Milhaud, who
adored Mexican food, but could only tolerate it in
small amounts.

Elgar: Pomp and Circumstance

Some music is pompous
Some music is wan
Some mentis are compos
Some mentis are non.

Enesco: Roumanian Rhapsody No. 1

Enesco fit cette rhapsodie
Vis-à-vis
La Roumanie.

Franck: Symphony in D Minor

César Franck composed the best he could.
His music sounds like Brahms, but not as good.

Gounod: Faust

I want you to know,
Monsieur Gounod,
  Your music suffers
When it's played too slow.

Grieg: Peer Gynt

Smoke for signals: that's okay,
Salmon's better that way.
   But when poisoning my lungs
It's time to say
   "Enough!"

Grieg: Piano Concerto in A Minor

Here, in a region
   Noted for intrigue,
Lived a Norwegian
   By the name of Grieg.

Handel: Water Music

Have any queries
  Turned up a scandal?
(A newspaper series
  On George Frederick Handel?)

Haydn: Symphony No. 88

Joseph Haydn, for a fee,
Wrote this symphony in G
(Number eighty-eight). He swore
He would stop at a hundred and four.

Haydn: Symphony No. 94
(Surprise)

Overtaken by a whim,
(Not unusual for him)
Haydn wrote a piece that's sym-
Phonic'ly surprising!

Ippolitoff-Ivanoff: Caucasian Sketches

This must be Rimsky-Korsakoff.
  No one else's
  Hyphenated
Name ends with an -off.

Kreisler: Caprice Viennoise

Saccharin's bad for your health,
   It is said.
Play this piece, daily,
   Instead.

Lalo: Symphonie Espagnole

Ed Lalo wrote a piece that I
   Like a lot,
Which he said was a symphony,
   Which it's not.
It's for orchestra, but that's not
   All it's got.
There's a violin grabbing the
   Solo spot,
Which it does when it finally
   Gets a shot. . .

Liszt: Hungarian Rhapsody No. 15

Rumors persist
That Franz Liszt
Never could resist:
Ladies to be kissed,
Vodka with a twist.

Mahler: Symphony No. 1

"Brevity's the soul of wit."
Mahler was well aware of it.
Still, he did not know when to quit.

Mendelssohn: A Midsummer Night's Dream

Mendel's son
  (Not troubled Felix,
The other one) spun
  The first double helix.

Mendelssohn: Symphony No. 4
(Italian)

Spaghetti
Is ready,
   So eat, everyone.
Any cognoscente
Knows al dente
   Means that it's done.

Mozart: Eine Kleine Nachtmusik

Eine
Kleine
Nachtmusik das ist,
Written
By Herr
Mozart, not by Liszt.

Mozart: Piano Sonata in C Major

Kids play this piece
Quite a lot.
Why this is so,
I completely forgot.

Mozart: Symphony No. 40

Give a hand
To the band
   Playing Mozart.
He wrote music both charming
   And witty.

"C'est jolie
Mon ami,"
   Just to quote Sartre.
I agree with my friend
   That it's pretty.

Mussorgsky: Pictures at an Exhibition

Was Mussorgsky called
Modest, or
Braggadocio?

Offenbach: Barcarolle

from TALES OF HOFFMANN

Offenbach
Was often in hock
For dental and doc-
tor bills.

Prokofieff: Peter and the Wolf

Sergei Prokofieff
Could barely read
The treble clef
Until he was
Past forty-seven.

Rachmaninoff: Piano Concerto No. 2

I know
A music buff
Who chooses "rock" because he
Isn't man enough.

Ravel: Bolero

If
You would like to know the easiest way
To drive someone really cra-
zy, all you have to do is play
Ravel's Bolero twenty times a day.

Ravel: La Valse

Tell
Mad'moiselle
That Ravel
Wants to sell
Their motel
To a chain.

Rimsky-Korsakoff: Scheherazade

"Nicholas,
   Let's say our divorce is off."
"Fine by me."
   Replied Rimsky-Korsakoff.

Rossini: Overture to
The Barber of Seville

I hate zucchini,
Veal scallopini,
Cold fettucini,
Rossini,
    And Pachelbel.

Saint-Saëns: The Swan
from CARNIVAL OF THE ANIMALS

**Why do composers think swans have class?
Have any seen one sticking out its ass?**

Schubert: Symphony No. 7

Schubert's Seventh has a scherzo
That only Toscanini played
Fast enough to sound vivace
    (A designation Schubert made).

If it's possible to sing it
  While mouthing lyrics like these,
Then the tempo's not vivace
  (And Schubert wasn't Viennese).

Schubert: Symphony No. 8
(Unfinished)

This is the symphony
   That Schubert wrote and never finished.
He should have edited
   The score before he was diminished.

Schumann: Träumerai

The worst
   Of Schumann's many faults
Was his appetite
   For unadulterated schmaltz.

Shostakovich: Symphony No. 7
(Leningrad)

Why tie a clove hitch
   When there's a bowline?
Ask Shostakovich,
   Whose trimaran was stolen.

Sibelius: Finlandia

What if Sibelius
   Had left Helsinki?
What if Mark Twain
   Had moved to New Rochelle?

Smetana: The Moldau

The man who wrote the Moldau
   (And our theme)
Bore the unlikely name
   Of sour cream.

Strauss: Don Juan

> The Strauss
> With musical talent,
> Sine qua non,
> Was not Johann.

Tchaikovsky: Piano Concerto No. 1

Tonight we love,
But tomorrow,
After dawn bathes the air,

The sun above
Will reveal
The flab and wrinkles everywhere.

Tchaikovsky: Symphony No. 4

"Repetition: is it required?"
Asked Tchaikovsky when he was hired.

Tchaikovsky: Symphony No. 6
(Pathétique)

If it sounds nice,
    Or better yet, sublime.
Then it sounds twice
    As nice the second time.

Wagner: Lohengrin

Doctors agree
They can't stop colds from occurring.

Vitamin C
Is a lot more reassuring.

Wagner: *Die Walküre*

Encumbered by sweaters,
I dodge Irish Setters
To bring you the letters
   That friends of yours wrote.

I need help locating
Some strong armor-plating
For Dobermans waiting
   To get at my throat.

Weber: Overture to Der Freischütz

Carl
Maria von
Weber
Would often
Snarl
At his noisy
Neighbor.

FOR THE BEST IN PAPERBACKS, LOOK FOR THE

In every corner of the world, on every subject under the sun, Penguin represents quality and variety—the very best in publishing today.

For complete information about books available from Penguin—including Pelicans, Puffins, Peregrines, and Penguin Classics—and how to order them, write to us at the appropriate address below. Please note that for copyright reasons the selection of books varies from country to country.

In the United Kingdom: For a complete list of books available from Penguin in the U.K., please write to *Dept E.P., Penguin Books Ltd, Harmondsworth, Middlesex, UB7 0DA.*

In the United States: For a complete list of books available from Penguin in the U.S., please write to *Dept BA, Penguin, Box 120, Bergenfield, New Jersey 07621-0120.*

In Canada: For a complete list of books available from Penguin in Canada, please write to *Penguin Books Ltd, 2801 John Street, Markham, Ontario L3R 1B4.*

In Australia: For a complete list of books available from Penguin in Australia, please write to the *Marketing Department, Penguin Books Ltd, P.O. Box 257, Ringwood, Victoria 3134.*

In New Zealand: For a complete list of books available from Penguin in New Zealand, please write to the *Marketing Department, Penguin Books (NZ) Ltd, Private Bag, Takapuna, Auckland 9.*

In India: For a complete list of books available from Penguin, please write to *Penguin Overseas Ltd, 706 Eros Apartments, 56 Nehru Place, New Delhi, 110019.*

In Holland: For a complete list of books available from Penguin in Holland, please write to *Penguin Books Nederland B.V., Postbus 195, NL-1380AD Weesp, Netherlands.*

In Germany: For a complete list of books available from Penguin, please write to *Penguin Books Ltd, Friedrichstrasse 10-12, D-6000 Frankfurt Main I, Federal Republic of Germany.*

In Spain: For a complete list of books available from Penguin in Spain, please write to *Longman, Penguin España, Calle San Nicolas 15, E-28013 Madrid, Spain.*

In Japan: For a complete list of books available from Penguin in Japan, please write to *Longman Penguin Japan Co Ltd, Yamaguchi Building, 2-12-9 Kanda Jimbocho, Chiyoda-Ku, Tokyo 101, Japan.*